Praying the Scriptures Journal

Trusting God with Your Children

JODIE BERNDT

ZONDERVAN

Praying the Scriptures Journal
Copyright © 2022 by Jodie Berndt

Requests for information should be addressed to:
Zondervan, *3900 Sparks Dr. SE, Grand Rapids, Michigan 49546*

Zondervan titles may be purchased in bulk for educational, business, fundraising, or sales promotional use. For information, please email SpecialMarkets@Zondervan.com.

ISBN 978-0-310-14345-1 (hardcover)
ISBN 978-0-310-14346-8 (ebook)

Library of Congress Cataloging-in-Publication Data on File

Cover design: Jamie DeBruyn
Interior design: Denise Froehlich

Printed in China

22 23 24 25 26 DSC 15 14 13 12 11 10 9 8 7 6 5 4 3 2 1

*My heart is stirred by a noble theme
as I recite my verses for the king; my
tongue is the pen of a skillful writer.*

PSALM 45:1

Contents

Praying for Your Child's Relationships

Praying for Your Child's Decisions

Praying for Your Child's Future

Introduction

If you remain in me and my words remain in you, ask
whatever you wish, and it will be done for you.

John 15:7

I've kept a journal for as long as I can remember. It's the place I record scriptural insights when the Holy Spirit reveals something fresh in the Bible, it's where I write about the ways I see God's hand at work, and—most of all—it's how I pray, spilling my heart onto the pages as I ask God to work in the lives of the people I love.

Praying the Scriptures Journal combines all of these things, and more. You'll find encouraging Scripture verses, time-tested prayer principles, and inspiring quotes from beloved authors. Plus, I'm sharing some of my most favorite scripture-prayers, verses that have anchored my faith as well as my parenting journey. It doesn't matter whether your child is a toddler, a teen, or an adult, God knows their needs. And when we allow his Word to shape our thoughts and desires, we can be confident that our prayers will line up with the good things he already has planned.

There's no "right" way to use this journal. You can pray through the sections in order, or turn straight to the one that addresses whatever need or concern you are currently facing. You can pour out your heart in entire sentences or use bullet points to keep track of your prayers. You can keep one journal for each of your children or bundle all of their lives in here together. Do what works for you.[1]

As you pray, remember to date your entries, and take time (I do this at the

---

1. If you are new to praying the scriptures, you'll find more information about this approach in my books, along with hundreds of additional prayer prompts and stories about how God has worked in families just like yours.

beginning of every month) to go back and see what God has done. Are there places where you've seen spiritual, physical, or emotional growth in your child? Friendships that have been forged or restored? Family circumstances where God is proving himself loving and faithful—even if the answer to your prayer has not come yet, or it doesn't look anything like you expect?

Our prayers release God's provision, and as we tell him our needs, thanking him for who he is and acknowledging what he has done, he promises to give us his peace.[2]

And one more thing: Don't be afraid to talk to God about the little details of your children's lives. Praying about the small stuff opens our eyes to the "ordinary" blessings God provides every day. As we thank God for these things, the path to his presence becomes familiar and worn. And then, when the bigger things come along—the painful rejection, the struggle with sin, the crisis of faith we didn't see coming—we can approach God with confidence, knowing that he understands, and that he will give us, and our children, mercy and grace for every need.[3]

With love,

Jodie

---

2. Philippians 4:6-7.
3. Hebrews 4:15-16.

PART 1

Praying for Your Child's Faith

Salvation

Whether you were raised in a Christian home or came to faith later in life, you want your children to have a vibrant, saving relationship with Jesus—one that impacts all that they think, say, and do. And it can be frustrating, sometimes, to realize that we can point our kids in the right direction, but we cannot *make* them love God. "No one," Jesus said, "can come to me unless the Father who sent me draws them" (John 6:44). Sometimes our children make a commitment to Christ at a young age, and we have the privilege of watching them mature in their faith. Other times, that decision happens much later. In both cases, though, we can be confident that God is always at work in their lives—and that he invites them to join him in accomplishing his best purposes (including their forever salvation!) through our prayers.

> *"Ask and it will be given to you; seek and you will find; knock and the door will be opened to you."*
>
> Matthew 7:7

This is the confidence we have in approaching God: that if we ask anything according to his will, he hears us. And if we know that he hears us—whatever we ask—we know that we have what we asked of him.

1 John 5:14–15

....
....
....
....
....
....
....
....
....
....
....
....
....
....
....
....
....
....
....
....
....
....
....
....
....

Prayer Principle

Praying for your children's salvation is asking God to give them the only gift that lasts forever.

"If you remain in me and my words remain in you, ask whatever you wish, and it will be done for you."

John 15:7

Three Prayers You Can Use for Salvation

Heavenly Father,

- May _____ confess with their mouth that "Jesus is Lord" and believe in their heart that you raised Jesus from the dead so that they will be saved. Romans 10:9
- Shine your light in _____'s heart to give the light of the knowledge of your glory displayed in the face of Christ. 2 Corinthians 4:6
- Open _____'s eyes and turn them from darkness to light, and from the power of Satan to God, so that they may receive forgiveness of sins and a place among those sanctified by faith in Christ. Acts 26:18

Write your own prayers here:

....
....
....
....
....
....
....
....
....
....
....
....
....
....
....
....
....

Prayer Principle

When you pray for your children's salvation, you can be confident that you are praying in accordance with God's will.

Assume a Posture of Prayer

1. Pray with an attitude of thanksgiving.

    "Devote yourselves to prayer, being watchful and thankful." Colossians 4:2

2. Build your faith.

    "For the eyes of the Lord are on the righteous and his ears are attentive to their prayer." 1 Peter 3:12

3. Be persistent.

    Jesus told his disciples "that they should always pray and not give up." Luke 18:1

What other actions can you take to prayer for your child's salvation? Write your thoughts and idea here:

....

....

....

....

....

....

....

....

....

....

....

....

....

....

....

....

....

God's giving is inseparably connected with our asking.

Andrew Murray

What's on your mind?

Three Prayers You Can Use for Salvation

Heavenly Father,

- Put people in _____'s life who will gently instruct them, and grant them repentance leading to a knowledge of the truth so that they will come to their senses and escape from the trap of the devil. 2 Timothy 2:25–26
- Don't let _____ be haunted by past mistakes. Remind _____ that if anyone is in Christ, the new creation has come; the old has gone, the new is here! 2 Corinthians 5:17
- Thank you for loving _____ so much that you gave your one and only Son, that whoever believes in him will not perish but have eternal life. John 3:16

....
....
....
....
....
....
....
....
....
....
....
....
....
....
....
....
....

Verses to Anchor Your Faith When You Find Yourself Waiting on God

- "Though [the revelation] linger, wait for it; it will certainly come and will not delay." Habakkuk 2:3
- "All your children will be taught by the LORD, and great will be their peace." Isaiah 54:13
- "I will repay you for the years the locusts have eaten. . . . and you will praise the name of the LORD your God, who has worked wonders for you." Joel 2:25–26

Write more of your favorite verses that support your children here:

....

....

....

....

....

....

....

....

....

....

....

....

....

....

....

....

....

....

Love of God's Word

I have hidden your word in my heart that I might not sin against you.

Psalm 119:11

Pray for a Love of God's Word

Heavenly Father,

- Let _____ keep your commands so that they will live; write them on the tablet of their heart. Proverbs 7:2–3
- Show _____ that your way is perfect and your Word is flawless, and that you shield all who take refuge in you. 2 Samuel 22:31
- Teach _____ that all Scripture is God-breathed and is useful for teaching, rebuking, correcting, and training in righteousness. 2 Timothy 3:16

....

....

....

....

....

....

....

....

....

....

....

....

....

....

....

....

....

....

In Luke 4, Satan finds Jesus, hungry and alone, in the desert. Jesus withstands the devil's schemes—not through intellectual prowess, physical strength, or willpower, but simply by knowing and using God's Word. Our children will face temptations and pressures; let's ask God to give them a love for, and knowledge of, his Word so they will be equipped to stand firm and enjoy the full and satisfying life Jesus came to provide.

....

....

....

....

....

....

....

....

....

....

....

....

....

....

....

....

....

....

....

....

....

....

> ### *Prayer Principle*
>
> Praying for your children to know, love, and use God's Word is the most effective way to pray for their protection.

Prompts for When You Don't Know What to Pray

- That your child would become aware of their spiritual need
- An openness to the Holy Spirit as their helper
- Friends and mentors who will point them toward Jesus
- Strong biblical teaching and a heart to embrace it
- A vibrant church community who will make your child feel welcome
- To delight in being shaped and taught by God's Word

Write your prayers here:

....
....
....
....
....
....
....
....
....
....
....
....
....
....
....
....
....
....
....

Inspiration: Share Scripture with Your Children

As parents, it's our job—and our privilege—to continually point our children toward Scripture, at all ages. "These commandments that I give you today are to be on your hearts," God says in Deuteronomy 6:6–7. "Impress them on your children. Talk about them when you sit at home and when you walk along the road, when you lie down and when you get up."

Ask God to show you the best way to share God's Word with your child, young or old, in this season.

....

....

....

....

....

....

....

....

....

....

....

....

....

....

....

....

....

....

....

As important as it is for us to pray, it is equally vital for our children to be equipped to withstand Satan's attacks. Their number one defense against the devil's pressures and temptations is the knowledge and prayerful application of Scripture.

What's on your mind?

Ask God to help your children recognize that his commands are not designed to limit their freedom but to set them up to flourish and live full lives!

> ## ⚜ *Prayer Principle*
>
> When you pray for your children to know and love Scripture, you are asking God to equip them for every good work.

Pray for a Love of God's Word

Heavenly Father,

- May _____ continue in what they have learned, knowing that the Holy Scriptures make us wise for salvation and equip us for every good work. 2 Timothy 3:14–17
- Do not let _____ merely listen to the Word, and so deceive themselves. Let them do what it says. James 1:22
- Give _____ a good heart so they will seize the Word and hold on, no matter what, sticking with it until there is a harvest. Luke 8:15 MSG

Write ways you have seen and ways you hope to see God's Word changing your child's life.

....

....

....

....

....

....

....

....

....

....

....

....

....

....

Child's Gifts

Each of you should use whatever gift you have received to serve others, as faithful stewards of God's grace in its various forms.

1 Peter 4:10

....
....
....
....
....
....
....
....
....
....
....
....
....
....
....
....
....
....
....
....
....

Prayerful Noticing

Ask God to open your eyes to the unique gifts he has given your child. Beside your child's name, list the strengths, gifts, talents, and abilities you recognize.

Note: You can use these spaces to repeat this practice with *one child* over time (noticing how his or her gifts express themselves in each new season), or use the spaces for *multiple children.*

Child's name:_____

Date: _____

Child's name:_____

Date: _____

Child's name:_____

Date: _____

Child's name:_____

Date: _____

Find an opportunity this week to tell your child what God showed you!

....

....

....

....

....

....

....

....

....

....

....

....

Every good and perfect gift is from above.

James 1:17

> ## Prayer Principle
>
> Ask God to show you the
> unique gifts he has given
> your children so you
> can see them as he sees
> them—as glimmering
> diamonds in the rough.

Just as God promised to give the Holy Spirit to the disciples, so he promises to give his Spirit to us. To discover more about how the Holy Spirit can work in your child's life, including the gifts he offers and how they should be used, consider these passages:

- John 14:25–27
- Acts 2:1–21
- 1 Corinthians 12
- Ephesians 4:1–16

....

....

....

....

....

....

....

....

....

....

....

....

....

....

....

....

....

....

....
....
....
....
....
....
....
....
....
....
....

⚜ *Prayer Principle*

Pray that your children will
use their gifts and talents to
accomplish God's purposes
rather than crave attention
from the world.

....
....
....
....
....
....
....
....

Big Idea

Dear God, let my children use their gifts for your glory. Help me understand how I can support them.

....
....
....
....
....
....
....
....
....
....
....
....
....
....
....
....
....
....
....
....
....
....
....
....
....

....
....
....
....
....
....
....
....
....
....
....

> ### *Prayer Principle*
>
> Praying for your children
> to recognize their gifts
> can help them gain a
> sense of destiny.

....
....
....
....
....
....
....
....
....
....
....

Perfect gifts in the hands of imperfect people can sometimes wind up looking more like liabilities than assets. As you consider your child's gifts and talents, ask God to show you how to help them learn to use these attributes wisely and well, in ways that will build up the body of Christ. Write your thoughts here:

Pray for Your Children's Gifts

Heavenly Father,

- Let _____ use their gifts to serve others, as a faithful steward of your grace in its various forms, so that in all things you will be praised and receive glory. 1 Peter 4:10–11
- Show _____ how to use their gifts and talents wisely, being faithful with the abilities you have entrusted to them. Matthew 25:21
- Thank you for the special gift you have given _____. Show them how this gift differs from the gifts you have given others, and let them be generous, diligent, and cheerful in using it. Romans 12:6–8

Child to Promote God's Kingdom

"You are the light of the world."

Matthew 5:14

....
....
....
....
....
....
....
....

⚜ *Prayer Principle*

When you pray for your children—in everything from their character to their future—you invite God to strengthen and equip them to promote his kingdom.

....
....
....
....
....
....
....
....

....
....
....
....
....
....
....
....
....
....
....
....

Big Idea

Ask God to reveal himself to your children as the light of the world and prompt them to follow him. That way, they will never walk in darkness but have the light of life to shine in the world.

What's on your mind?

How to Use Our Gifts

Ephesians 4:12 says that the gifts God gives us are meant to build up the body of Christ, but these gifts can also be used for self-serving and worldly purposes. Notice the gifts you identified in your child and pray that they will be used to shine the spotlight on God.

....

....

....

....

....

....

....

....

....

....

....

....

....

....

....

....

....

....

....

....

....

....

Prayer Principle

When you pray for your children to promote God's kingdom, you must be prepared to let them respond to his call—even if it means incurring risk or making great sacrifices.

Big Idea

As we pray, let's ask God to fill our children with the heart and mind of Christ so they can reach out to others with his life-changing love.

Lord, make my heart brave so that nothing—from the fear of sickness or persecution, to the threat of ostracism from their peers—will hinder my willingness to pray for my children to proclaim your faithfulness and promote your kingdom.

Strengths to Pray For

Pray that your children will embody the strengths and attributes of the real-life heroes of the Bible.

- Paul's boldness
- Esther's courage
- King David's heart for God
- Stephen's spiritual sensitivity
- Noah's out-on-a-limb faithfulness
- Abraham's obedience
- Daniel's moral purity
- Ruth's loyalty

....

....

....

....

....

....

....

....

....

....

....

....

....

....

....

....

....

Pray for Your Children to Promote God's Kingdom

Heavenly Father,

- Let _____'s light shine before others, that people will see their good deeds and praise you, our Father in heaven. Matthew 5:16
- I pray that _____ would always be prepared to give an answer to everyone who asks about the reason for their hope, and that they would speak with gentleness and respect. 1 Peter 3:15
- Let _____ sing of your great love forever; let them make known your faithfulness through all generations. Psalm 89:1

....
....
....
....
....
....
....
....
....
....
....
....
....
....
....
....
....
....

PART 2

Praying for Your Child's Character

Wisdom and Discernment

If any of you lacks wisdom, you should ask God, who gives generously to all without finding fault, and it will be given to you.

James 1:5

The reason godly wisdom is so important is that it opens our minds to the way God works and allows us to respond to life with God's perspective.

....
....
....
....
....
....
....
....
....
....
....
....
....
....
....
....
....
....
....
....
....
....
....
....
....
....
....

....

....

....

....

....

....

....

....

                                                        ....

                                                        ....

Prayer Principle   ....

When you ask God to give   ....
your children wisdom and   ....
discernment, you are asking   ....
him to enable them to see   ....
the world through his eyes—   ....
and to think, speak, act, and   ....
respond accordingly.   ....

                                                        ....

....

....

....

....

....

....

....

....

....

Pray for Wisdom for Your Child

- It helps them manage their time effectively. Psalm 90:12
- It makes them good listeners. Proverbs 1:5
- It provides direction and purpose in life. Proverbs 3:5–6
- It opens the door to happiness, true riches, and a long and pleasant life. Proverbs 3:13–17
- It offers insight into the character of others and protection from evil. Proverbs 7:4–5
- It leads to strong, joy-filled family relationships. Proverbs 10:1
- It has the power to save their lives. Ecclesiastes 7:12 NLT

Write your prayers here:

....

....

....

....

....

....

....

....

....

....

....

....

....

....

....

....

Pray for Your Child's Wisdom and Discernment

Heavenly Father,

- Fill _____ with the knowledge of your will through all the wisdom and understanding that the Spirit gives so that they may live a life worthy of you, Lord, and please you in every way—bearing fruit and growing in knowledge of you. Colossians 1:9–10
- Give _____ wisdom. Thank you that you give generously to everyone without finding fault. Help _____ to believe and not doubt, and give them singleness of mind and stability in all that they do. Help them make good decisions. James 1:5–8
- Cause _____ to fear you, as this is the beginning of wisdom. Cause _____ to know you and to understand your perspective on any situation. Grant wisdom, that _____ may enjoy many days. Proverbs 9:10–11

....

....

....

....

....

....

....

....

....

....

....

....

....

....

Heart for Service

Let us not become weary in doing good, for at the proper time we will reap a harvest if we do not give up.

Galatians 6:9

Big Idea

Jesus made the connection between love and sacrificial service in John 15:12–13: "Love each other as I have loved you. Greater love has no one than this: to lay down one's life for one's friends."

Write ways your children have shown God's love in their lives.

....

....

....

....

....

....

....

....

....

....

....

....

....

....

....

....

....

....

....

....

....

....

Prayer Principle

Praying for a servant's heart means praying that your child will get excited about helping others flourish.

Pray to Nurture a Heart for Service in Your Child

Heavenly Father,

- Don't let _____ become weary in doing good, for at the proper time they will reap a harvest if they do not give up. Galatians 6:9
- Thank you that _____ is your handiwork, created in Christ Jesus to do good works, which you prepared in advance. Ephesians 2:10
- Motivate _____ to serve wholeheartedly, as if they were serving you, not people, knowing that you will reward everyone for whatever good they do. Ephesians 6:7–8

....

....

....

....

....

....

....

....

....

....

....

....

....

....

....

....

....

....

....

Kindness and Compassion

Therefore, as God's chosen people, holy and dearly loved, clothe your-selves with compassion, kindness, humility, gentleness and patience.

Colossians 3:12

....
....
....
....
....
....
....
....
....
....

Prayer Principle

Praying for your children's lives to be marked with compassion opens the door for God to work on their attitudes as well as their actions.

....
....
....
....
....
....
....
....
....
....

*One of my favorite prayers comes from Ezekiel 11:19.
Here God tells the Israelites he will "give them an
undivided heart and put a new spirit in them" and
"remove from them their heart of stone and give them
a heart of flesh." God does not change; he is the same
yesterday and today and forever. What he did for the
Israelites, he can do for our children, turning hardened
hearts of stone into compassionate hearts of flesh.*

What's on your mind?

Pray for Your Child's Kindness and Compassion

Heavenly Father,

- Clothe _____ with compassion, kindness, humility, gentleness, and patience. Colossians 3:12
- Do not let any unwholesome talk come out of _____'s mouth, but only what is helpful for building others up according to their needs, that it may benefit those who listen. Ephesians 4:29
- When _____ is hurt or offended, may they respond with kindness and compassion, forgiving others just as in Christ you forgave them. Ephesians 4:32

....

....

....

....

....

....

....

....

....

....

....

....

....

....

....

....

Self-Control, Diligence, and Self-Discipline

No discipline seems pleasant at the time, but painful. Later on, however, it produces a harvest of righteousness and peace for those who have been trained by it.

Hebrews 12:11

*It's ultimately the Holy Spirit's heart work,
not a parent's hard work, that produces
Christlike character in our children.*

Jeannie Cunnion, *Mom Set Free*

....

....

....

....

....

....

....

Prayer Principle

When you pray for your
children to learn things like
diligence and self-control, you
are asking God to give them
attributes that are absolutely
essential to their future
happiness and success.

....

....

....

....

....

....

Pray for Self-Control, Diligence, and Self-Discipline

Heavenly Father,

- Show _____ that no discipline seems pleasant at the time, but painful—but that your training and correction will produce a harvest of righteousness and peace in their lives. Hebrews 12:11
- *(For a daughter)* Help _____ to be self-controlled and pure, to be busy at home, to be kind, and—if she marries—to be subject to her husband, so that no one will malign the Word of God. Titus 2:5
- *(For a son)* Help _____ to exercise self-control. Let him show integrity, seriousness, and soundness of speech that cannot be condemned, so that those who oppose him may be ashamed because they have nothing bad to say about him. Titus 2:6–8

Write additional prayers here:

....

....

....

....

....

....

....

....

....

....

....

....

....

....

Honesty and Integrity

"If you hold to my teaching, you are really my disciples. Then you will know the truth, and the truth will set you free."

John 8:31–32

Our ability to ruin our children is nothing compared to God's power to redeem them. He is not surprised by anything they do, and having started a good work in their lives, he promises to complete it (Philippians 1:6).

Prayer Principle

Very often our greatest
growth comes from our
greatest failures.

Pray for Honesty and Integrity

Heavenly Father,

- A good person produces good things from the treasury of a good heart, and an evil person produces evil things from the treasury of an evil heart. Work in _____'s heart so that good things will flow out. Luke 6:45 NLT
- Cause _____ to put off falsehood and speak truthfully, for we are all members of one body. Ephesians 4:25
- Keep _____ from deceitful ways. Teach them to choose the way of faithfulness and equip them to hold fast to your statutes so that they will never be put to shame. Psalm 119:29–31

....
....
....
....
....
....
....
....
....
....
....
....
....
....
....
....

Praying for a Humble, Teachable Heart

Remind the people to be subject to rulers and authorities, to be obedient, to be ready to do whatever is good, to slander no one, to be peaceable and considerate, and always to be gentle toward everyone.

Titus 3:1–2

May _____take your yoke and learn from you, for you are gentle and humble in heart. Matthew 11:29

> ### Prayer Principle
>
> Asking God to give our children a teachable heart equips them to receive his correction in life.

Pray for a Humble, Teachable Heart

Heavenly Father,

- May _____ be submissive to authority, obedient, and ready for every good work. May they speak evil of no one, avoid quarreling, be gentle, and show perfect courtesy toward all people. Titus 3:1–2 ESV

- Let _____ give you praise and glory for their talents and abilities, knowing that everything they have comes from you. 1 Chronicles 29:11–14

- May _____ delight in your Word, since it is useful for teaching, rebuking, correcting, and training in righteousness. Equip _____ for every good work. 2 Timothy 3:16–17

Write additional prayers here:

....

....

....

....

....

....

....

....

....

....

....

....

....

....

....

....

....
....
....
....
....
....
....
....
....
....

⚜ *Prayer Principle*

Don't wait for a crisis to
prompt you to pray for
your child; ask God to work
in the everyday things.

....
....
....
....

....
....
....
....
....
....
....
....
....
....
....
....

Pray for Compassion and Kindness

Heavenly Father,

- May _____ follow your example, being compassionate and gracious, slow to anger, and abounding in love. Psalm 103:8
- Cause _____ to be like you are—kind to the ungrateful and the wicked, doing good to them without expecting to get anything back. Luke 6:35
- Comfort _____ in all their troubles so that they can comfort others in their time of need. 2 Corinthians 1:4

....

....

....

....

....

....

....

....

....

....

....

....

....

....

....

....

....

Praying Through Anger
to Compassion

Better to be patient than powerful; better to have self-control than to conquer a city.

Proverbs 16:32 NLT

> ## Prayer Principle
>
> When you ask God to demolish something ugly in your child's life, name the stronghold and trust him to pull it down.

How to Pray

As we pray for our children, let's point them toward the solution outlined in Romans 12:17–21. Let's pray:

- that they would behave honorably, never repaying anyone evil for evil, but being careful to do the right thing;
- that they would do everything in their power to live at peace with others, knowing that when they do their part, the results are up to God;
- that they would never try to take revenge, but that they would let God—whose wrath always includes his mercy—be the one to repay those who deserve it;
- that they would channel their anger into blessings, looking for ways to provide good things for those who have wronged them, that their enemies might be ashamed of their past actions;
- that they would never be controlled by anger or let evil get the best of them, but that they would be empowered by the Holy Spirit to overcome evil with good.

....

....

....

....

....

....

....

....

....

....

....

Be angry, and yet do not sin; do not let the sun go down on your anger,
and do not give the devil an opportunity.

Ephesians 4:26–27 NASB

What's on your mind?

Pray for Your Child to Move Through Anger to Compassion

Heavenly Father,

- Teach _____ how to be just like you—compassionate and gracious, slow to anger, abounding in love and faithfulness. Psalm 86:15
- Don't let _____ be like a fool who gives full vent to their rage, but cause them to be wise and bring calm. Proverbs 29:11
- When _____ gets angry, do not let them sin or let the sun go down on their anger and thereby give the devil a foothold. Ephesians 4:26–27

....
....
....
....
....
....
....
....
....
....
....
....
....
....
....
....
....
....

> ## Prayer Principle
>
> Serving others frees our children from the burden of self-absorption.

Pray for an Outlook Focused on Others

Heavenly Father,

- Fill _____ with your Holy Spirit. Let their words and deeds be marked by love, joy, peace, patience, kindness, goodness, faithfulness, gentleness, and self-control. Galatians 5:22–23 NLT
- Let _____ put you first, others second, and themselves third. May they love you with all their heart, soul, and mind and love others as themselves. Matthew 22:37–39
- Turn _____'s heart toward your statutes and not toward selfish gain. Psalm 119:36

Write more prayers here that focus on your child's healthy attitude toward others:

....

....

....

....

....

....

....

....

....

....

....

....

....

....

....

PART 3

Praying for Your Child's Health, Safety, and Well-Being

Physical Health, Safety, and Security

In peace I will lie down and sleep, for you alone, LORD, make me dwell in safety.

Psalm 4:8

....
....
....
....
....
....
....
....
....
....
....
....
....
....
....
....
....
....
....
....
....
....
....
....
....
....
....

> ## Prayer Principle
>
> Prayers for your children's safety may be rooted in the certainty that God loves them and that the Lord is always alert and on the job.

Big Idea

Jesus didn't just help the sick children; his ministry included words of hope and encouragement for their hurting and weary parents:

- "Don't be afraid," he told the synagogue ruler (Mark 5:36).
- "Woman, you have great faith," he said to the Canaanite (Matthew 15:28).
- "Everything is possible for one who believes," he promised the long-suffering father of the demon-possessed boy (Mark 9:23).

Write prayers of hope and encouragement for your children:

....
....
....
....
....
....
....
....
....
....
....
....
....
....
....
....
....

Three Prayers for Yourself

Heavenly Father,

- Thank you for telling us we should always pray and not give up. Help me not to become weary as I pray for _____, but to remember that your timing is perfect. Luke 18:1; Galatians 6:9
- May I speak with gracious words that are sweet to the soul and healing to the bones. Proverbs 16:24
- You tell us to confess our sins to each other and pray for each other so that we may be healed, and that the prayer of a righteous person is powerful and effective. Search my heart, remove my sin, and equip me to pray with power. James 5:16; Psalm 139:23

....

....

....

....

....

....

....

....

....

....

....

....

....

....

....

....

....

God doesn't just want to heal your child;
he wants to take care of you too.

What's on your mind?

This is what the LORD . . . says: I have heard your prayer and seen your tears; I will heal you.

2 Kings 20:5

....
....
....
....
....
....
....
....
....
....
....
....
....
....
....
....
....
....
....
....
....
....
....
....
....
....

Big Idea

When I suffered a major loss I struggled to understand, God comforted me with this Scripture:

> *"My thoughts are not your thoughts, neither are your ways my ways,"
> declares the LORD. "As the heavens are higher than the earth, so are
> my ways higher than your ways and my thoughts than your thoughts."
> (Isaiah 55:8–9)*

....

....

....

....

....

....

....

....

....

....

....

....

....

....

....

....

....

....

....

Praying for Health, Safety, and Well-Being

- I pray that _____ will enjoy good health and that all will go well with them. 3 John 2
- *(For a son)* Be with _____. Protect him from fear. Strengthen him, help him, and uphold him. Isaiah 41:10
- *(For a daughter)* May _____ praise you in her inmost being, knowing that you forgive all her sins and heal all her diseases. Psalm 103:1–3

....
....
....
....
....
....
....
....
....
....
....
....
....
....
....
....
....
....
....
....

Spiritual Protection

"Lead us not into temptation, but deliver us from the evil one."

Matthew 6:13

Clothing a Child with the Armor of God

The best way I've found to get my kids outfitted for the battles they'll face is to clothe them in the "armor of God" Paul described in Ephesians 6:10–18. First, I pray that they will be strong in the Lord rather than relying on their own strength of mind or will. Then I put the armor on them, piece by piece: the belt of truth to stabilize them in the face of lies and deception; the breastplate of righteousness so that their behavior will line up with their identity in Christ; shoes that will anchor them in God's peace and allow them to move forward as they carry the gospel; the shield of faith to extinguish Satan's flaming arrows and inspire them to action; the helmet of salvation to cover their minds and guard their identity in Christ. And finally, I pray that my children will take up the sword of the Spirit, which is God's Word. I ask the Lord to keep them alert and ready to use Scripture as they pray, doing so like Paul said: on all occasions, with all kinds of requests, and for all the Lord's people.

....

....

....

....

....

....

....

....

....

....

....

....

....

....

Big Idea

Asking God to protect our children may be a parent's most oft-repeated prayer. But more often than not, our prayers center around *physical* protection, ignoring the invisible—but incredibly potent—dangers in the *spiritual* realm. And these unseen threats are very real. As Ephesians 6:12 reads, "For our struggle is not against flesh and blood, but against the rulers, against the authorities, against the powers of this dark world and against the spiritual forces of evil in the heavenly realms."

Write prayers of protection for your children:

....

....

....

....

....

....

....

....

....

....

....

....

....

....

....

....

....

....

*There are two equal and opposite errors into which
our race can fall about the devils. One is to disbelieve
in their existence. The other is to believe, and to feel
an excessive and unhealthy interest in them. They
themselves are equally pleased by both errors and hail
a materialist or a magician with the same delight.*

C. S. Lewis, *The Screwtape Letters*

....
....
....
....
....
....
....
....
....
....
....
....
....
....
....
....
....
....
....
....

....

....

....

....

....

....

....

....

....

⚜ *Prayer Principle*

You can pray for your
children's spiritual
protection with faith and
joy, knowing that Jesus
is greater than any of the
dark forces in their world.

....

....

....

....

....

....

....

....

....

Pray for Spiritual Protection

Heavenly Father,

- Keep _____ from all harm. Watch over their life; watch over their coming and going, both now and forevermore. Psalm 121:7–8
- Lead _____ not into temptation, but deliver them from the evil one. Matthew 6:13
- Put a hedge of protection and blessing around _____ and everything they have. Job 1:10

....
....
....
....
....
....
....
....
....
....
....
....
....
....
....
....
....
....
....
....

Identity and Emotional Health and Well-Being

I pray that you, being rooted and established in love, may have power, together with all the Lord's holy people, to grasp how wide and long and high and deep is the love of Christ, and to know this love that surpasses knowledge—that you may be filled to the measure of all the fullness of God.

Ephesians 3:17–19

Prayer Principle

Praying for your children to be rooted and built up in Christ's love equips them to flourish emotionally—even during times of uncertainty and disappointment.

A Prayer for a Child's Contentment and Joy when Facing Challenges

Pray that your child will know...

1. God is good.
2. God is in charge.
3. God loves them and wants what's best for them.

....
....
....
....
....
....
....
....
....
....
....
....
....
....
....
....
....
....
....
....
....
....
....
....

....

....

....

....

....

....

....

....

....

....

....

....

> ### *Prayer Principle*
>
> God is in the business of transformation, and he has promised to renew us—body, mind, and spirit—day by day.

....

....

....

....

....

....

....

....

I waited patiently for the LORD;
he turned to me and heard my cry.
He lifted me out of the slimy pit,
out of the mud and mire;
he set my feet on a rock
and gave me a firm place to stand.
He put a new song in my mouth, a hymn of praise to our God.

Psalm 40:1-3

....
....
....
....
....
....
....
....
....
....
....
....
....
....
....
....
....
....
....
....

Prayer Principle

When you pray your child through a mental or emotional illness, don't let shame or fear keep you from enlisting trusted prayer partners to help carry your burden.

Heavenly Father,

- When our family suffers, let us not be ashamed. Instead, let us be confident in your ability to guard whatever we entrust to you, including our child's emotional health. 2 Timothy 1:12
- Help me believe that I will receive what I ask you for. Equip me to forgive people (including myself), even as you forgive me. Mark 11:24–25
- Thank you for taking what is meant for harm and using it for good. Let us not be afraid but trust you to provide for our children. Genesis 50:20–21

Write additional prayers for yourself here:

....

....

....

....

....

....

....

....

....

....

....

....

....

....

....

....

Pray for Your Child's Identity and Emotional Well-Being

Heavenly Father,

- May _____ be still and know that you are God. Psalm 46:10
- *(For a son)* Cause _____ to revere your name, and may the sun of righteousness rise in his life, with healing in its rays. Malachi 4:2
- *(For a daughter)* Lead _____ by ways she has not known; guide her along the unfamiliar [treatment] paths. Turn her darkness into light, and make the rough places smooth. Do not forsake her. Isaiah 42:16

....
....
....
....
....
....
....
....
....
....
....
....
....
....
....
....
....
....
....
....

Protection from Harm

The angel of the LORD encamps around those who fear him.

Psalm 34:7

Prayer Principle

Asking God to put his angels in charge of your child's safety encompasses more than just physical protection. We can trust him to stand guard over their hearts and minds too.

Protection from Harm: Prayers You Can Use for Yourself

Heavenly Father,

- When I am weak or frightened, help me remember that your grace is sufficient for me and that your power is made perfect in weakness. 2 Corinthians 12:9
- I know you will carry my children close to your heart. Be my shepherd, too, and lead me as I pray for them. Isaiah 40:11
- Help me not to be anxious about anything, but in every situation, by prayer and petition, let me present my requests to you. And may your peace, which passes all understanding, guard my heart and mind in Christ Jesus. Philippians 4:6–7

....

....

....

....

....

....

....

....

....

....

....

....

....

....

....

....

....

Listen for the voice of Jesus calling you to himself, "Come to me, all you who are weary and burdened, and I will give you rest" (Matthew 11:28).

Prayer Principle

When your child is in a crisis situation, how you pray and what you do reveals what you believe about God.

Protection from Harm: Prayers You Can Use for Your Child

Heavenly Father,

- May your faithfulness be _____'s shield and rampart. Do not let them fear the terror of night or the arrow that flies by day. Psalm 91:4–5
- Let no harm befall _____. Command your angels concerning _____ to guard them in all their ways [body, mind, and spirit]. Psalm 91:10–11
- Equip _____ to be on guard, to stand firm in the faith, to be courageous, and to be strong. 1 Corinthians 16:13

....
....
....
....
....
....
....
....
....
....
....
....
....
....
....
....

Season of Challenge or Crisis

"Do not fear, for I have redeemed you;
I have summoned you by name; you are mine.
When you pass through the waters,
I will be with you;
and when you pass through the rivers,
they will not sweep over you.
When you walk through the fire,
you will not be burned;
the flames will not set you ablaze."

Isaiah 43:1–2

> ## Prayer Principle
>
> The most effective prayers stem from the knowledge that God is absolutely, totally, 100 percent in control.

If your child is in a crisis situation—whether because of bad choices they've made or the result of circumstances beyond their control—don't give up on God. As Job 42:2 reminds us, God can do all things and no purpose of his can be thwarted. Rather than second-guessing God's design, let's remember that he holds the future—and that our job is not to be anxious, but to be strong, take heart, and wait for the Lord.

God's Promise

"Call to me and I will answer you and tell you great and unsearchable things you do not know."

Jeremiah 33:3

What's on your mind?

"Perfect love drives out fear."

1 John 4:18

Prayer Principle

Trusting God when we don't know what the future holds opens the door to peace.

Prayers for Healing

Heavenly Father,

- Send out your Word and heal _____ ; rescue them from the grave. Psalm 107:20
- Help _____ not to lose heart. When they feel like they are outwardly wasting away, renew them day by day. 2 Corinthians 4:16
- Cause _____ to keep your Word in their heart, knowing that it brings life and health to the whole body. Proverbs 4:20–22

Write prayers of healing that have helped you through difficult times:

....

....

....

....

....

....

....

....

....

....

....

....

....

....

....

....

....

....

Praying for Children in Crisis

Heavenly Father,

- When trouble, hardship, persecution, danger, or any need arises, let _____ remember that we are "more than conquerors" and that nothing can separate us from the love of God that is in Christ Jesus our Lord. Romans 8:35–39
- May _____ be alert and of sober mind so they can stand firm in suffering. Restore _____ and make them strong, firm, and steadfast. 1 Peter 5:8–10
- Create a pure heart in _____. Do not cast them from your presence; instead, restore joy and make them willing to obey you. Psalm 51:10–12

Write additional prayers for your children here:

....
....
....
....
....
....
....
....
....
....
....
....
....

PART 4

Praying for
Your Child's
Relationships

Relationship with Christ

So then, just as you received Christ Jesus as Lord, continue to live your lives in him, rooted and built up in him, strengthened in the faith as you were taught, and overflowing with thankfulness.

Colossians 2:6–7

Lord, make him a man of God; Lord, make her a woman of God.

What's on your mind?

Praying for Relationship with Christ

Heavenly Father,

- Tune _____'s ears to hear your voice so that, as Samuel did when he was a boy, they will invite you to speak and then listen to your words. 1 Samuel 3:9–10
- Allow _____ to be rooted and established in love. Give them power to grasp how wide and long and high and deep is the love of Christ. Ephesians 3:17–18
- Cause _____ to trust you and never be shaken. Psalm 125:1

....

....

....

....

....

....

....

....

....

....

....

....

....

....

....

....

....

....

Relationship with Parents

Honor your father and your mother, as the LORD your God has commanded you, so that you may live long and that it may go well with you in the land the LORD your God is giving you.

Deuteronomy 5:16

Prayers for Parents

Dear God,

- Let us make the most of the time we have with our children; grant us all an eagerness to spend time together.
- Show me how to point my children toward Jesus Christ.
- Help me see discipline as a gift to my young children; grant me wisdom to know how to counsel and come alongside them when they are older.

Write additional prayers for yourself and your spouse here:

....

....

....

....

....

....

....

....

....

....

....

....

....

....

....

....

....

Prayer Principle

Praying for your children to love, respect, trust, and obey you helps pave the way for them to love, respect, trust, and obey their heavenly Father.

Turn the hearts of the parents to their children, and the hearts of the children to their parents.

Malachi 4:6

What's on your mind?

When we pray for our children's relationship with us, we invite God to unleash his blessings in their lives, fulfilling his promise that things "may go well" with them (Ephesians 6:3). What a privilege it is to know that our expressions of love for our children can pave the way for God to reveal himself as their heavenly Father! And the more our kids see us depending on God for things like wisdom, guidance, and strength, the more they will understand that it's not about our abilities (because we will never do everything "right"); it's all about God's provision and grace!

....

....

....

....

....

....

....

....

....

....

....

....

....

....

....

....

Fathers, do not embitter your children, or they will become discouraged.

Colossians 3:21

Praying for Your Child's Relationship with You

- Help me preach your Word and be prepared in season and out of season. Show me how to correct, rebuke, and encourage _____ — with great patience and careful instruction. 2 Timothy 4:2
- Teach me how to set a godly example for _____, and equip them to be like King Solomon, who walked before you in integrity of heart and uprightness, even as his father David did. 1 Kings 9:4
- Cause _____ to obey all your commands, including the one about honoring parents, and remain in your love so that your joy will be in them and their joy will be complete. John 15:10–11

Relationships with Siblings

How good and pleasant it is when God's people live together in unity!

Psalm 133:1

When God is at work in our children's lives, there is always reason to hope. If you are in the place where you are wondering if things will ever get better in your household, let Paul's words in Romans 15:13 be your prayer: "May the God of hope fill you with all joy and peace as you trust in him, so that you may overflow with hope by the power of the Holy Spirit."

Big Idea

God is always at work—even when we cannot see what he is doing. Ask God to help you recall the times when he came through for you in ways that you weren't expecting.

What's on your mind?

Pray for Relationships Between Siblings

Heavenly Father,

- Give _____ endurance, encouragement, and a spirit of unity as they follow Jesus, so that with one heart and mouth they may glorify you. Romans 15:5–6
- Do not let any unwholesome talk come out of _____'s mouth, but only what is helpful for building others up according to their needs, that it may benefit those who listen. Ephesians 4:29
- Cause _____ to be devoted to one another in brotherly love, honoring one another above themselves. Romans 12:10

....

....

....

....

....

....

....

....

....

....

....

....

....

....

....

....

....

....

....

Relationships with Friends

As iron sharpens iron, so one person sharpens another.

Proverbs 27:17

Prayer Principle

Praying for your children's friendships involves praying that they will be the kind of friends you want them to have.

Big Idea

Don't be surprised if God works in a way you didn't see coming. Our job is to ask; God's job is to answer. What have you asked God for as it relates to your child? How were you surprised by his great love for you and your child?

....

....

....

....

....

....

....

....

....

....

....

....

....

....

....

....

....

....

....

....

....

....

....

Three Ways We Can Pray for Our Children's Friendships

Pray for constancy. The Bible showcases friendships marked by loyalty, dependability, and faithfulness. Let's ask God for these things.

Pray for transparency. Let's pray for honest friendships, people with whom our kids can admit mistakes and find restoration, forgiveness, and genuine love.

Pray for Christian friends. Friendship with other believers—the "fellowship of the Holy Spirit" Paul talked about in 2 Corinthians 13:14—brings connection not just on the natural level but also in the deepest recesses of the soul.

Write additional prayers here:

....

....

....

....

....

....

....

....

....

....

....

....

....

....

Prayer Principle

We are created for connection. Ask God to bless your child with rich and meaningful relationships.

Praying for Relationships with Friends

Heavenly Father,

- I pray that _____ will choose friends carefully, for the way of the wicked leads them astray. Proverbs 12:26
- Surround _____ with friends who will sharpen them as iron sharpens iron. Proverbs 27:17
- Let _____ flee the evil desires of youth and pursue righteousness, faith, love, and peace, enjoying the companionship of those who call on you out of a pure heart. 2 Timothy 2:22

....

....

....

....

....

....

....

....

....

....

....

....

....

....

....

....

....

....

Relationships with Teachers, Coaches, and Bosses

Have confidence in your leaders and submit to their authority, because they keep watch over you as those who must give an account. Do this so that their work will be a joy, not a burden, for that would be of no benefit to you.

Hebrews 13:17

Prayer Principle

Asking God to give your children a teachable spirit involves allowing him to use their mistakes and failures as stepping-stones on the path to victory.

You know our needs even before we ask you,
Lord (Matthew 6:8). May my child be mentored
and taught by the people you choose.

What's on your mind?

Praying for Relationships with Teachers, Coaches, and Bosses

Heavenly Father,

- Turn _____'s ear toward wisdom and their heart toward understanding. Give _____ a teachable spirit, one that calls out for insight and searches for it as for hidden treasure. Proverbs 2:2–4

- Cause _____ to have confidence in teachers, coaches, and bosses and submit to their authority, since they will be accountable to you for the job they do. May _____ make their work a joy, not a burden. Hebrews 13:17

- Prompt _____ to show proper respect to everyone, love others, respect you, and honor those in authority. 1 Peter 2:17

....

....

....

....

....

....

....

....

....

....

....

....

....

....

....

....

Romantic Relationships:
Dating and Marriage

Note: If your children are not yet in this season of life, you can use this space to pray for their future.

Above all else, guard your heart, for everything you do flows from it.

Proverbs 4:23

Prayer Principle

When you don't see eye to eye with your child about a romantic relationship—dating, engagement, or marriage—ask God to give you his perspective.

When my child feels lonely as a single person, may they know your heal-ing comfort and be filled with the double joy of fellowship with other believers and with you (2 Corinthians 1:4; 1 John 1:3 MSG).

....

....

....

....

....

....

....

....

....

....

....

....

....

....

....

....

....

....

....

....

....

....

....

....

....

....

....

....

....

Prayer Principle

When you pray for your child's marriage partner, it's okay to be specific, but be prepared for God to surprise you.

Praying for Your Child's Current or Future Romantic Relationships

- As I pray for _____'s marital status, give me the oil of gladness instead of mourning, and a garment of praise instead of despair. Isaiah 61:3
- Whether _____ is married or single, help them recognize that marriage and singleness are both gifts from you. 1 Corinthians 7:7
- Do not let _____ be yoked together with an unbeliever in marriage, for what fellowship can light have with darkness? Instead, let their heart be drawn to someone who lives and walks with you. 2 Corinthians 6:14–16

....

....

....

....

....

....

....

....

....

....

....

....

....

....

....

....

....

....
....
....
....
....
....
....
....
....
....
....
....
....

Prayer Principle

Ask God to connect your child with someone who makes them better, someone who spurs them on toward love and good deeds.

....
....
....
....
....
....
....
....
....
....

Relationships in Christian Community

Let us consider how we may spur one another on toward love and good deeds, not giving up meeting together, as some are in the habit of doing, but encouraging one another—and all the more as we see the Day approaching.

Hebrews 10:24-25

Fellowship has become a churchy word that suggests basements and red punch and awkward conversation. But it is really a word for the flow of rivers of living water between one person and another, and we cannot live without it.

John Ortberg, *The Me I Want to Be*

....
....
....
....
....
....
....
....
....
....
....
....
....
....
....
....
....
....
....
....

....

....

....

....

....

....

....

....

....

....

Prayer Principle

If your child is not going to church, ask God to prompt someone to invite them.

....

....

....

....

....

....

....

....

....

....

....

....

....

....

....

....

As I pray for my child to find friends and fellowship, help me remember that you have promised never to leave us or forsake us (Hebrews 13:5). Thank you for being our forever friend.

Praying for Connection to Church

Heavenly Father,

- As we pray for _____'s involvement in church, help us hold tightly to hope, knowing that you are faithful. Let us consider how we can spur them on toward love and good deeds. Hebrews 10:23–24
- Don't let _____ give up meeting together with other believers, even if some of their friends quit going to church, but show them how they can love and encourage others. Hebrews 10:25
- Let _____ be like King David, rejoicing with those who say, "Let us go to the house of the Lord." Psalm 122:1

Write additional prayers here:

....
....
....
....
....
....
....
....
....
....
....
....
....
....
....
....

PART 5

Praying for Your Child's Decisions

Technology

Whatever is true, whatever is noble, whatever is right, whatever is pure, whatever is lovely, whatever is admirable—if anything is excellent or praiseworthy—think about such things.

Philippians 4:8

Technology is the number one reason parents believe raising kids is more complicated than it was in the past. We can't control how and where technology will impact our children's lives, but we can move from panic to peace when we remember that God is working with us to shape our kids' hearts and teach them to use technology wisely and well.

What's on your mind?

Big Idea

While there's no one-size-fits-all approach to putting technology in its proper place (one where its use facilitates human connection, sparks creativity, and enriches our understanding of the world), a few common-sense considerations can help.

1. Let's cut back on our own screen time.
2. Let's view technology use in light of our bigger-picture goals for our family.
3. When our children are young, let's engage with them when they use screens.
4. Let's take our cue from the apostle Paul, who wrote what may be the very best parenting advice when it comes to our children and technology: "Devote yourselves to prayer, being watchful and thankful" (Colossians 4:2).

....
....
....
....
....
....
....
....
....
....
....
....
....
....

> **Prayer Principle**
>
> God doesn't want us to be worried or scared; he reveals things so we can pray.

We are meant not just for thin, virtual connections but for visceral, real connections to one another in this fleeting, temporary, and infinitely beautiful and worthwhile life.

Andy Crouch, *The Tech-Wise Family*

....
....
....
....
....
....
....
....
....
....
....
....
....
....
....
....
....
....
....
....
....
....
....
....
....

Prayer Principle

Ask God to put a filter
on your child's heart
so that they can see
technology through
heavenly eyes.

Pray for Your Child's Use of Technology

Heavenly Father,

- May we live with a heart of integrity in our house. Don't let _____ set anything worthless before their eyes. Psalm 101:2–3 CSB

- Give _____ alertness and a sober mind as they use technology. Protect them from the enemy that wants to devour them. 1 Peter 5:8

- As _____ uses computers, phones, and other devices, may they only be drawn to that which is true, noble, right, pure, lovely, admirable, excellent, and praiseworthy. Philippians 4:8

....
....
....
....
....
....
....
....
....
....
....
....
....
....
....
....
....
....

Sexual Purity

Do you not know that your bodies are temples of the Holy Spirit, who is in you, whom you have received from God? You are not your own; you were bought at a price. Therefore honor God with your bodies.

1 Corinthians 6:19–20

....
....
....
....
....
....
....
....
....
....

Prayer Principle

God's heart is to redeem, and his power often shines brightest in the darkness.

....
....
....
....
....
....
....
....
....
....
....
....
....
....
....
....
....

Do not conform to the pattern of this world, but be transformed by the renewing of your mind.

Romans 12:2

....
....
....
....
....
....
....
....
....
....
....
....
....
....
....
....
....
....
....
....
....
....
....
....
....

When my child is caught in sexual sin, show them the kindness that leads them to repentance. Put people in their life who will remind them of this truth: nothing can separate them from your love.

....

....

....

....

....

....

....

....

....

....

....

....

....

....

....

Prayer Principle

Shame can be
the single biggest
hindrance to our child's
connection with Christ.

....

....

....

....

....

....

....

....

....

....

Praying for Sexual Purity

Heavenly Father,

- When _____ experiences conviction of sin, remind them that you are the God who brings the dead back to life and who creates new things—including reputations and purity—out of nothing. Romans 4:17 NLT
- Equip _____ to be self-controlled and live in holiness and honor—not in passionate lust, like the example so often set by people who do not know you. 1 Thessalonians 4:4–5
- Do not let any part of _____'s body become an instrument of evil to serve sin. Instead, may _____ use their whole body as an instrument to do what is right for the glory of God. Romans 6:12–13 NLT

Write additional prayers here:

....
....
....
....
....
....
....
....
....
....
....
....
....
....

Substance Use and Abuse

Wine is a mocker and beer a brawler; whoever is led astray by them is not wise.

Proverbs 20:1

Promises of God

- God's mercies never fail; they are new every morning. (Lamentations 3:22–23)
- Jesus' peace replaces our fear. (John 14:27)
- God strengthens us when we are weak. (Isaiah 40:29)

....

....

....

....

....

....

....

....

....

....

....

....

....

....

....

....

....

....

....

....

....

....

Do not let my child conform to the world's pattern of drug use, but transform and renew their minds so they will be able to recognize and approve of your good, pleasing, and perfect will (Romans 12:2).

What's on your mind?

Big Idea

Substance abuse can hold our children captive, but they aren't the only ones who suffer. We can find ourselves in a prison of shame and confusion. As parents, let's come alongside one another and be quick to extend love and grace to those who are hurting.

....
....
....
....
....
....
....
....
....
....
....
....
....
....
....
....
....
....
....
....
....
....

Prayer Principle

We must be faithful
in love and expectant
in prayer as we wait
for God to work in our
child's life.

Pray for Your Child's Use of Drugs or Alcohol

Heavenly Father,

- Let _____ thirst for a drink from your river of delights rather than for anything that alcohol or drugs offer, for with you is the fountain of life. Psalm 36:8–9
- Teach _____ what is best; direct them in the way they should go. Cause _____ to pay attention to your commands so they will experience peace like a river and well-being like the waves of the sea. Isaiah 48:17–18
- Cause _____ to live a decent life for all to see, not participating in darkness but being clothed with the presence of Christ. Romans 13:13–14 NLT

....

....

....

....

....

....

....

....

....

....

....

....

....

....

....

....

Recovery from Addiction

He has sent me to bind up the brokenhearted, to proclaim freedom for the captives and release from darkness for the prisoners.

Isaiah 61:1

Helpful Resource

As you pray for a child who is caught in the grip of addiction, it can help to remember the "Three Cs" from Al-Anon, an international support group for families and friends of problem drinkers:

- I didn't *cause* it.
- I can't *control* it.
- I can't *cure* it.

Write your thoughts here:

....
....
....
....
....
....
....
....
....
....
....
....
....
....
....
....
....
....

Big Idea

God's love is bigger and more powerful than any addiction.

··

··

··

··

··

··

··

··

··

☙ *Prayer Principle*

God's heart is to heal and deliver our children; our prayers are part of the rescue operation.

··

··

··

··

··

··

··

··

··

··

··

··

··

··

O blessed Lord, you ministered to all who came to you: Look with compassion upon all who through addiction have lost their health and freedom. Restore to them the assurance of your unfailing mercy; remove from them the fears that beset them; strengthen them in the work of their recovery; and to those who care for them, give patient understanding and persevering love. Amen.

The Book of Common Prayer

What's on your mind?

Praying for Your Child to Be Released from the Bondage of Addiction

Heavenly Father,

- Open _____'s eyes; free them from the captivity of addiction; release them from the dungeon of darkness. Isaiah 42:6–7
- Do not let _____ be tempted beyond what they can bear. When they are tempted by alcohol, drugs, food, or any other addiction, provide a way out, so that they can endure it. 1 Corinthians 10:13
- Remind _____ that you have been tempted in every way and that you empathize with our human weakness. Cause _____ to draw near to you and approach your throne of grace with confidence so that they will find mercy and grace to help in their time of need. Hebrews 4:15–16

....
....
....
....
....
....
....
....
....
....
....
....
....
....
....

Sin to Be Exposed

You may be sure that your sin will find you out.

Numbers 32:23

My child's sins—even the secret ones—are revealed in the light of your presence. Teach my child to make the most of this time and grow in wisdom (Psalm 90:8, 12).

....

....

....

....

....

....

....

....

....

⚜ *Prayer Principle*

Concealing sin never
ends well, but confession
leads to mercy.

....

....

....

....

....

....

....

....

....

....

....

Big Idea

*"You intended to harm me, but God intended it for good to accomplish
what is now being done, the saving of many lives."*
Joseph to his brothers in Genesis 50:20

Write about a time when what seemed like a bad situation turned out to
be for your good.

....

....

....

....

....

....

....

....

....

....

....

....

....

....

....

....

....

....

....

....

....

....

*God, I trust you to redeem my child's life and use even the darkest
situation to bring about something good.*

Whoever conceals their sins does not prosper, but the one who confesses and renounces them finds mercy.

Proverbs 28:13

What's on your mind?

Praying for Your Child's Sin to Be Exposed

Heavenly Father,

- Cause _____ to renounce secret and shameful ways. Do not let them use deception or do anything to distort your Word. 2 Corinthians 4:2
- Let _____ have nothing to do with the fruitless deeds of darkness, but rather expose them, realizing it is shameful even to mention what the disobedient do in secret. Ephesians 5:11–12
- When _____ is caught in sin, have mercy. Wash away all iniquity and cleanse them from sin, giving them a clean heart and a spirit that is willing to obey you. Psalm 51:1–2, 10–12.

....
....
....
....
....
....
....
....
....
....
....
....
....
....
....
....

Your Prodigal Child

I will give them a heart to know me, that I am the LORD. *They will be my people, and I will be their God, for they will return to me with all their heart.*

Jeremiah 24:7

Big Idea

As we partner with God and pray for our prodigals, let's keep a few key points in mind:

- First, God knows our pain. He knows exactly how it feels to have a child walk away.
- Next, God loves our children, even more than we do.
- Third, God has given us "great and precious promises"—promises designed to enable us to live godly lives and pray with confidence (2 Peter 1:3–4).
- And finally, as we consider how to behave toward our children, particularly as we try to navigate the thin space between discipline and grace and as we wrestle with our own feelings of anger and hurt, let's take our cue from our heavenly Father. We all need God's mercy and grace. And God, in turn, has shown us exactly how to live. We must, he says, "Be joyful in hope, patient in affliction, faithful in prayer" (Romans 12:12).

....

....

....

....

....

....

....

....

....

....

....

....

....

> ## Prayer Principle
>
> God knows what it's like to grieve over a prodigal child—and to rejoice over their return.

Praying for Your Prodigal Child

Heavenly Father,

- No one can come to Christ unless the Father draws them. Draw _____, Lord. John 6:44
- Summon _____ by name. Strengthen them, even though they do not acknowledge you, so they will know that you alone are the Lord. Isaiah 45:4–6
- Grant _____ repentance, and lead them to know the truth. May they come to their senses and escape from the trap of the devil, who has taken them captive to do his will. 2 Timothy 2:25–26

....

....

....

....

....

....

....

....

....

....

....

....

....

....

....

PART 6

Praying for Your Child's Future

Purpose in Life

Note: Whatever age your child is—new to this world or older than you were when that child was born—God holds your child's future and invites you to partner with him in prayer.

"For I know the plans I have for you," declares the LORD, "plans to prosper you and not to harm you, plans to give you hope and a future."
Jeremiah 29:11

Big Idea

Author Jean Fleming (*A Mother's Heart*) recommends regular times of prayer and planning for each child. As we bring our children before the Lord, she says we should:

- *acknowledge* God's hand on their lives, even before they were born;
- *admit* any areas we resent in the way God put our children together;
- *accept* God's design for each child, thanking him for how he or she is made;
- *affirm* God's purpose in creating our children for his glory; and
- *ally* ourselves with God in his plans for their lives.

....

....

....

....

....

....

....

....

....

....

....

....

....

....

....

....

....
....
....
....
....
....
....
....
....
....

Prayer Principle

God loves your children and has a unique plan for each of their lives.

....
....
....
....
....
....
....
....
....
....
....
....

For you created my inmost being;

you knit me together in my mother's womb . . .

Your eyes saw my unformed body;

all the days ordained for me were written in your book

before one of them came to be.

Psalm 139:13, 16

....

....

....

....

....

....

....

....

....

....

....

....

....

....

....

....

....

....

....

....

....

....

....

....

Pray for Your Child's Purpose

Heavenly Father,

- You have plans for _____, plans to prosper them and not to harm them, plans to give them hope and a future. Listen to _____ when they pray. Cause _____ to seek you—and find you—with their whole heart. Jeremiah 29:11–13
- Let _____ live carefully and wisely, making the most of every opportunity and understanding what your will is. Ephesians 5:15–17
- Work in _____ to will and to act to fulfill your good purpose. Philippians 2:13

Write additional prayers here:

....
....
....
....
....
....
....
....
....
....
....
....
....
....
....
....

Your Child's Future

"What no eye has seen, what no ear has heard, and what no human mind has conceived"—the things God has prepared for those who love him.

1 Corinthians 2:9

*When it comes to praying about your child's future—
whether you need discernment as you discipline,
wisdom in selecting the right college, peace about
a chosen career path, or guidance and protection
in adulthood—God's promise in Jeremiah 29:11–13
serves as a beautiful launching pad for our prayers:*

"For I know the plans I have for you," declares the LORD, "plans to prosper you and not to harm you, plans to give you hope and a future. Then you will call on me and come and pray to me, and I will listen to you. You will seek me and find me when you seek me with all your heart."

Prayer Principle

When we pray for our child, we partner with God as he accomplishes his good plans for their lives.

For it is God who works in you to will and to act in order to fulfill his good purpose.

Philippians 2:13

What's on your mind?

A God Who Listens

God has promised to listen to us. I love how the New Living Translation renders Psalm 116:2:

> Because he bends down to listen,
> I will pray as long as I have breath.

God bends down to listen. He invites us to pray—now and always.

....
....
....
....
....
....
....
....
....
....
....
....
....
....
....
....
....
....
....

Prayer from Numbers 6:24–26

The beautiful prayer that Moses spoke over the Israelites became our go-to blessing during our kids' growing-up years. It's still my favorite. Borrow this one for your own family if you like—and as you do, know that I have prayed it for you:

> The LORD bless you
> and keep you;
> the LORD make his face shine on you
> and be gracious to you;
> the LORD turn his face toward you
> and give you peace.

Pray for Your Child's Future

Heavenly Father,

- Let _____ be glad for all that you are planning. May _____ be joyful in hope, patient in affliction, and faithful in prayer. Romans 12:12
- Fulfill your purpose in _____. Give them a rich and satisfying life. John 10:10 NLT
- Fill _____ with knowledge and depth of insight to discern what is best in their future schooling, career choices, and family life. May _____ be pure and blameless, filled with the fruit of righteousness that comes through Jesus, so as to bring glory to your name. Philippians 1:9–11

....

....

....

....

....

....

....

....

....

....

....

....

....

....

....

....

Child's Marriage

He who finds a wife finds what is good and receives favor from the LORD.

Proverbs 18:22

....
....
....
....
....
....
....
....
....
....
....
....
....
....
....
....
....
....
....
....
....
....
....
....
....

Big Idea

Pray that your children will marry people who love God with all their heart, soul, mind, and strength and who will love their neighbors as themselves (Mark 12:29–31). Rather than choosing a particular *person* for your child to marry, it's a good idea to pray for specific *character traits* or *attributes* in the spouse God has in mind.

Write your prayers here:

....
....
....
....
....
....
....
....
....
....
....
....
....
....
....
....
....
....
....
....

"Well," my father said, "from the time you were a teenager, we prayed a two-part prayer. First, we asked God to put a hedge around your emotions and not permit you to be drawn to anyone he didn't want you to be with. And second, we asked that when the Lord sent the one he had chosen, the Holy Spirit would rule in your heart. We prayed that the peace of Christ would rule in your heart—sort of like an umpire in your decision."

....

....

....

....

....

....

....

....

....

....

....

....

....

....

....

....

....

....

....

....

> ## *Prayer Principle*
>
> **As God to put a hedge of protection around your child's heart.**

Praying for Your Child's Marriage

Heavenly Father,

- Cause _____ to be willing to wait for your perfect timing in finding a marriage partner, even as Jacob waited seven years to marry Rachel. And, as you did for Jacob, let the waiting period seem to go by quickly. Genesis 29:20
- *(For a son)* Let _____ be a considerate husband who treats his wife with respect so that nothing will hinder his prayers. Let him love his wife in the same way that Christ loved the church, being willing to give himself up for her. 1 Peter 3:7; Ephesians 5:25
- *(For a daughter)* Let _____ be a wife who is worthy of respect, not a malicious talker but temperate and trustworthy in everything. Let her be willing to submit to her husband as she does to the Lord. 1 Timothy 3:11; Ephesians 5:22

Young Marriage

A man will leave his father and mother and be united to his wife, and the two will become one flesh. This is a profound mystery.

Ephesians 5:31–32

Prayer Principle

When your children get married, your prayers take on a new dimension. Now you're not just praying for him or for her; you're also praying for them.

Pillars of Prayer for Your Child's Marriage

1. *Make it not "all about me."* In an age when marriage is often seen as a means to happiness and personal fulfillment, it can be easy to adopt a self-centered attitude. I want my kids' relationships to be marked by humility and an eagerness to serve one another.

2. *Let them be each other's best friend.* I pray that my children and their spouses will be the kind of friend who "loves at all times" (Proverbs 17:17) and that they will sharpen one another "as iron sharpens iron" (Proverbs 27:17), making each other wiser, better, and stronger.

3. *May they be quick to forgive.* I'm asking God to fill their marriage with the 1 Corinthians 13 kind of love, the kind that is patient, kind, and keeps no record of wrongs.

4. *May their love and their lives be filled with the Holy Spirit.* When we start with an infilling of God's Spirit, it informs how we speak to one another, how we worship, and how able we are to give thanks. With a Spirit-filled marriage, all good things are possible.

....

....

....

....

....

....

....

....

....

....

....

....

Prayer Principle

We do the praying; God does the changing.

Marriage brings you into more intense proximity to another human being than any other relationship can. Therefore, the moment you marry someone, you and your spouse begin to change in profound ways, and you can't know ahead of time what these changes will be. So you don't know, you can't know, who your spouse will actually be in the future until you get there.

Timothy Keller with Kathy Keller, *The Meaning of Marriage*

....
....
....
....
....
....
....
....
....
....
....
....
....
....
....
....
....
....
....

Pray for Your Child's Young Marriage

The following prayers are excerpted from "The Celebration and Blessing of a Marriage" in the *Book of Common Prayer*. My husband and I prayed these words over our children during their wedding ceremonies, and we continue to pray these same blessings for them today. The references that accompany each prayer represent my own thoughts about how and where these prayers reflect Scripture.

> Look with favor upon the world you have made, and for which your Son gave his life, and especially upon _____ and _____, whom you make one flesh in Holy Matrimony. Amen.
>> Leviticus 26:9; John 3:16; Mark 10:8
>
> Give _____ and _____ wisdom and devotion in the ordering of their common life, that each may be to the other a strength in need, a counselor in perplexity, a comfort in sorrow, and a companion in joy. Amen.
>> Proverbs 27:17; Proverbs 27:9; 2 Corinthians 1:4; Ecclesiastes 4:9–10; Psalm 149:5
>
> Grant that their wills may be so knit together in your will, and their spirits in your Spirit, that _____ and _____ may grow in love and peace with you and one another all the days of their life. Amen.
>> Psalm 40:8; Galatians 5:25; 2 Corinthians 13:11; Psalm 23:6

....

....

....

....

....

....

....

....

Troubled Marriage or Divorce

Be patient, bearing with one another in love.

Ephesians 4:2

> ## Prayer Principle
>
> When your children go through painful trials, ask God to use their suffering to produce perseverance, character, and hope.

Prayers for *Yourself* in the Midst of Your Child's Troubled Marriage or Divorce

Heavenly Father,

- As I speak to and pray for _____ and _____, may the words of my mouth and the meditation of my heart be pleasing in your sight. Psalm 19:14
- When _____ causes grief to our family, help me to extend forgiveness, comfort, and love so that Satan might not outwit us. 2 Corinthians 2:7–11
- Out of the depths I cry to you, Lord. Hear my voice and let your ears be attentive to my cry for mercy. Psalm 130:1–2

....

....

....

....

....

....

....

....

....

....

....

....

....

....

....

Big Idea

You might not know how to pray, but the Holy Spirit does—and he is always praying for us, even with groanings that can't be put into words.

Write your thoughts here:

....

....

....

....

....

....

....

....

....

....

....

....

....

....

....

....

....

....

....

....

....

....

....

....

....

....

....

....

....

....

....

....

....

....

....

....

....

....

Prayer Principle

When you pray for your child's troubled marriage, remember that his or her spouse is not the enemy.

....

....

....

....

....

....

....

....

....

....

....

Pray for Your Child's Troubled Marriage or Divorce

Heavenly Father,

- May _____ and _____ be completely humble and gentle. May they be patient, bearing with one another in love. Ephesians 4:2
- May _____ be quick to listen, slow to speak, and slow to become angry. James 1:19
- Help _____ and _____ to make allowance for each other's faults and forgive each other when they are offended. Colossians 3:13

....

....

....

....

....

....

....

....

....

....

....

....

....

....

....

....

....

....

....

....

When Your Children
Have Children

I will pour out my Spirit on your offspring, and my blessing on your descendants.

Isaiah 44:3

Prayer Principle

Ask God to provide friends
and mentors who will lovingly
point your grandchildren
toward Christ.

Pray Psalm 139 during your children's pregnancies, asking God to fill them with peace about their babies, knowing that he is forming them in wonderful ways and recording every day of their lives, even before they are born.

Praying for Children's Children: For You

Heavenly Father,

- May your love remain with me forever as I fear you; may your salvation extend to my children's children. Psalm 103:17 NLT
- May I never forget your laws and the good things you have done; equip me to teach them to my children and grandchildren. Deuteronomy 4:9
- Be with me even when I am old and gray; let me declare your power to the next generation and your mighty acts to all who are to come. Psalm 71:18

....

....

....

....

....

....

....

....

....

....

....

....

....

....

....

....

....

Praying for Your Children's Children

Heavenly Father,

- Make your word a lamp to _____'s feet and a light for their path. Psalm 119:105
- Clothe _____ with compassion, kindness, gentleness, humility, and patience. Colossians 3:12
- May _____ grow as Jesus did, in wisdom and stature and in favor with God and man. Luke 2:52

Write additional prayers here:

....

....

....

....

....

....

....

....

....

....

....

....

....

....

....

....

....

....